PRAYER JOURNAL

30 DAYS ON WISDOM

Artwork by Ruth Chou Simons

Written by Erika Allen

:: CROSSWAY

ESV Prayer Journal: 30 Days on Wisdom

Copyright © 2023 by Crossway

Published by Crossway
1300 Crescent Street
Wheaton, Illinois 60187

Cover Design: Ruth Chou Simons

Artwork: Ruth Chou Simons

First printing 2023

Printed in China

Trade paperback ISBN: 978-1-4335-8857-0

Crossway is a publishing ministry of Good News Publishers

RRDS 34 33 32 31 30 29 28 27 26 25 24 23
14 13 12 11 10 9 8 7 6 5 4 3 2 1

Contents

Introduction

Give me understanding, that I may keep your law
and observe it with my whole heart.

PSALM 119:34

Have you ever been reading the Bible when a familiar word or phrase jumped out at you and you suddenly realized, "I have no idea what that actually means?" Or perhaps you've been asked to define or explain a biblical concept and were surprised you were unable to do so?

Some concepts and words are found so often in the pages of Scripture that it is clear they are foundational to the Christian faith—but many times we lack a clear understanding of, or the ability to articulate, what those words mean. This can be true even for those of us who grew up in the faith or have been immersed in the Bible for many years. And it can be difficult to admit to ourselves, and especially to others, that we are clueless.

But understanding the basic themes of the Bible is crucial if we are to move on to the solid food of Scripture. One thing these journals are for, then, is to provide clear, concise definitions and teaching on foundational themes of the Bible that we often talk about but perhaps don't fully understand.

Sometimes the reason we gloss over particular words or phrases in the Bible is because they are difficult to wrap our minds around. Perhaps the concept is so mysterious that we don't know quite where to start. Or maybe we were taken aback by what we read because it was offensive to our human nature: "Surely this verse can't mean that?"

The second purpose of this journal is to help us study God's Word, and some of its crucial themes, *prayerfully*. We typically think of Bible study and prayer as two equally important, but quite distinct, spiritual disciplines. But the two are closely linked. It has been said that the Bible is God's speaking to us, while prayer is our speaking to God. **This journal aims to help you approach Bible study as a conversation with the God who delights in revealing himself to his people.**

The journal will prompt you to pray through several passages of Scripture, asking God himself to give you understanding and to shape your theology on the key theme being studied. By praying the Scriptures while we seek to understand them, we will gain wisdom in how to apply God's Word rightly. Our theology will not merely be hypothetical or abstract but will have a direct impact on how we live.

How to Use This Journal

This journal is designed to guide you through a study on the theme of wisdom over the course of six weeks. Each week focuses on one specific passage that deals with this key biblical theme. Thus by the end of six weeks you will have studied six passages that deal with wisdom.

Each **week** includes five days' worth of teaching, prayer prompts, and space for you to journal. Each **day** includes two types of content to help guide your time in prayerful Bible study:

1. A few short paragraphs of clear teaching on a specific phrase or aspect of that week's passage
2. A brief prompt to help guide your prayer over the passage

Additionally, a total of seven overviews are provided, one that serves as an introduction to the foundational biblical theme and six that are based on each week's passage of Scripture. Often these overviews will focus on the context and background of the passage being studied.

As you begin every day, open your Bible to that week's verse or passage and read it carefully, letting it shape and inform the content of your prayers. Hebrews 4:12 tells us that God's Word is "living and active." A passage will continue to speak to us every time it is read. Ask the Lord to help you grow in your understanding of the passage and to know how to apply its teaching.

Let your prayers be honest and open. If a verse you read seems confusing or unsettling—or even makes you angry—talk with God about that! Acknowledge that you are struggling and ask for his help. The truth is, we need the Lord's help even to know what questions to ask. Approaching Bible study prayerfully keeps us mindful of our utter dependence on the Lord.

Pray and study the Scriptures with the awareness that, as we do so, God will graciously shine light on areas in our lives in which we need to repent and grow. At times it will feel daunting to make the changes the Lord requires. But as we strive for obedience and holiness, we do so with the mind-blowing knowledge that, in the ultimate sense, God is completely pleased with us already, because we bear the name of his precious Son, our Savior Jesus. In Jesus we need never fear condemnation (Rom. 8:1).

Wisdom

DEFINITION: *The ability to apply knowledge, sound judgment, and discernment in such a way that honors and reflects God. True wisdom is not something we possess naturally or can acquire on our own. It is a gift of the Spirit, who is given to us so "that we might understand the things freely given us by God" (1 Cor. 2:12).*

The Bible teaches that wisdom begins with the fear of the Lord, which includes recognizing him for who he is and responding accordingly:

> *The fear of the LORD is the beginning of knowledge;*
> *fools despise wisdom and instruction. (Prov. 1:7)*

We grow in wisdom in two primary ways. The first is by knowing God's Word and in humility submitting to its authority. The second is by relying on the Spirit, who teaches us how to understand God's Word properly and how to apply it to specific situations.

The Purpose of Wisdom

In Mark 12 a scribe takes note of Jesus' wisdom and is captivated by it. He asks Jesus, "Which commandment is the most important of all?" And Jesus answered,

> The most important is, "Hear, O Israel: The Lord our God, the Lord is one. And you shall love the Lord your God with all your heart and with all your soul and with all your mind and with all your strength." The second is this: "You shall love your neighbor as yourself." There is no other commandment greater than these. (Mark 12:28–31)

The Great Commandment is straightforward and clear. But we quickly realize that neither love for God nor love for others comes naturally to us. Regardless of our good intentions, when our own desires or comforts are threatened, our first instinct is to look out for—to love—ourselves.

Therefore we need help and guidance to know how to love God and others. We need *wisdom*, which God graciously provides through his Word and Spirit. Over the next few weeks we will study six passages that help us see that the fundamental reasons the Bible tells us to pursue wisdom are so that we can (1) faithfully love, honor, and obey the Lord and (2) love and serve others.

WEEK 1

Deuteronomy 4:5–9

WEEK 1

*⁵ See, I have taught you statutes and rules, as the L*ORD *my God com-manded me, that you should do them in the land that you are entering to take possession of it. ⁶ Keep them and do them, for that will be your wisdom and your understanding in the sight of the peoples, who, when they hear all these statutes, will say, "Surely this great nation is a wise and understanding people." ⁷ For what great nation is there that has a god so near to it as the L*ORD *our God is to us, whenever we call upon him? ⁸ And what great nation is there, that has statutes and rules so righteous as all this law that I set before you today?*

⁹ Only take care, and keep your soul diligently, lest you forget the things that your eyes have seen, and lest they depart from your heart all the days of your life. Make them known to your children and your children's children.

DEUTERONOMY 4:5–9

A Wise and Understanding People

As the people of Israel prepare to enter the Promised Land, Moses stands before them and recounts their history up to this point. Israel is reminded not only of her rebellion against God and the penalty for her disobedience but also of God's steadfast love and care for her, even in the wilderness.

Deuteronomy 4, which we will be studying this week, is a transitional chapter. The focus of the book changes from history to exhortation: in light of God's unwavering faithfulness, Israel must respond with gratitude and wholehearted obedience (Deut. 4:1).

Deuteronomy 4:5–9, the specific verses we will focus on, highlight the interconnectivity between wisdom and God's Word: it is by keeping God's commands that his people receive and display wisdom and understanding (v. 6). Israel's submission to God's authority will set his people apart from those who currently occupy the land that Israel is about to possess. Israel will be renowned as a "great nation" and a "wise and understanding people" (v. 6). And, when this occurs, they will glorify the God of Israel and be a blessing to those around them.

The New Testament picks up this theme in 1 Peter 2, where we who follow Jesus are told that we have been called to

> proclaim the excellencies of him who called you out of darkness into his marvelous light. . . . Keep your conduct among the Gentiles honorable, so that when they speak against you as evildoers, they may see your good deeds and glorify God on the day of visitation. (1 Pet. 2:9, 12)

God's purpose for us, as it was for Israel, is to point others to him. One way we do this is by exercising wisdom.

Day 1

As we seek to grow in wisdom, our first step as believers is to grow in our knowledge of Scripture. Before we can obey God's commands, we have to know what they are! Likewise, we need to understand what his character is like if we are to imitate it. The Bible is God's *revelation* of himself to us: it is through the Bible that we know who he is and what he demands.

Psalm 111:10 declares,

> The fear of the LORD is the beginning of wisdom;
>   all those who practice it have a good understanding.

We fear the Lord—we treat him with the honor and reverence he deserves—by knowing and obeying his Word.

Our passage this week begins with Moses' telling the people of Israel, "I have taught you statutes and rules, as the LORD my God commanded me, that you should do them in the land that you are entering to take possession of it" (Deut. 4:5). The Lord has graciously revealed his will to us in Scripture. It is as we read and learn and meditate on his Word that we grow in wisdom and understanding.

Read Deuteronomy 4:5–9 carefully today. Spend time reflecting on the relationship between wisdom and the Word of God. Ask the Lord to give you a greater love for and desire to know the Bible.

Day 2

If we are to be wise, we not only must know God's Word but must be changed by it so that it shapes the way we live. In Romans 12:2 the Christian is instructed to "be transformed by the renewal of your mind, that by testing you may discern what is the will of God, what is good and acceptable and perfect."

It can be tempting to think that we have a good handle on the Bible if we are able to quote a lot of verses about many different topics. But each of us must evaluate our knowledge of Scripture and ask, Is it truly changing the way I think, speak, and act? We know that our minds are being renewed by the Spirit when God's thoughts about any given subject begin to override our own—when our responses begin to reflect Jesus more and more.

When our hearts and minds are transformed by God's Word, the world takes notice. Moses says to Israel in Deuteronomy 4:6,

Keep [God's statutes and rules] and do them, for that will be your wisdom and your understanding in the sight of the peoples, who, when they hear all these statutes, will say, "Surely this great nation is a wise and understanding people."

The wisdom and understanding that come from knowing and keeping God's Word are to be used for the benefit of those who do not know him. Godly wisdom is a powerful evangelistic tool. As you pray today, meditate on verse 6. Ask God to reveal specific areas in which your viewpoint or attitude needs to reflect more closely the teachings of the Bible.

Day 3

The imaginary gods of Israel's neighbors were temperamental beings who were kept happy through strange and sometimes awful means. The favor of these false gods was never promised to those who served them; their followers could only hope for the best. Such gods were impersonal and uncaring. They were not deities who could be approached in order to receive compassion or mercy.

Israel's relationship with her God stood in stark contrast to that false belief. Moses reminds the people of the uniqueness of the covenant between God and Israel: "What great nation is there that has a god so near to it as the LORD our God is to us, whenever we call upon him?" (Deut. 4:7). Unlike her unbelieving neighbors, Israel was not left alone to navigate life on her own—and neither are we. Our God is near, even more so now that "the Word became flesh and dwelt among us" (John 1:14).

James 1:5 promises,

> If any of you lacks wisdom, let him ask God, who gives generously to all without reproach, and it will be given him.

Our God faithfully answers us when we call out to him. This sets us apart from the rest of the world, as our wisdom comes from outside us. It comes from the one who is wisdom.

As you pray today, spend time reflecting on Deuteronomy 4:7. Is there an issue in your life about which you are desperate for discernment? Are you confused or discouraged? Call out to God and ask for wisdom.

Day 4

In Deuteronomy 4:8 God asks through his servant Moses,

> What great nation is there, that has statutes and rules so righteous as all this law that I set before you today?

Through his infallible Word God tells us what is morally good and true. As such, the Bible is our only source of absolute authority. In Psalm 119:105 the psalmist declares, "Your word is a lamp to my feet and a light to my path." God's Word is what enables us to see clearly in a world darkened by sin. We cannot find our way without it.

The statutes and rules given to Israel were a tremendous gift. As the recipient of God's law, she knew what true righteousness looked like. Likewise, it is because of our relationship with God and his speaking to us through his Word that we are able to discern good from evil. We measure every situation that arises, and every decision that has to be made, against his Word.

Because God's commands often stand in such stark contrast to that which the world defines as good and true, sometimes we are tempted to view his commands as burdensome rather than a gift. But Deuteronomy 4:8 reminds us of the beauty and truth of God's Word. There is no righteousness—no true and lasting goodness—apart from it.

As you pray today, reflect on verse 8. Thank God for the instruction and guidance he provides in Scripture.

Day 5

King Solomon was famed for his unrivaled wisdom. But 1 Kings 11:1–6 reveals the shocking extent to which he abandoned that wisdom by the end of his reign:

> King Solomon loved many foreign women, along with the daughter of Pharaoh: Moabite, Ammonite, Edomite, Sidonian, and Hittite women, from the nations concerning which the Lord had said to the people of Israel, "You shall not enter into marriage with them, neither shall they with you, for surely they will turn away your heart after their gods." Solomon clung to these in love. He had 700 wives, who were princesses, and 300 concubines. And his wives turned away his heart. For when Solomon was old his wives turned away his heart after other gods, and his heart was not wholly true to the Lord his God, as was the heart of David his father. For Solomon went after Ashtoreth the goddess of the Sidonians, and after Milcom the abomination of the Ammonites. So Solomon did what was evil in the sight of the Lord and did not wholly follow the Lord, as David his father had done.

So many things compete for our attention and affection. Much of what the world deems as good and true and beautiful resonates with our sin nature, and often we must fight against our own hearts and minds in order to submit to God's authority. And so our passage this week ends with an admonition. Pray Deuteronomy 4:9 back to God today. Ask him to keep your heart and mind focused squarely on him—that you will not be deceived or enticed by things contrary to his Word.

WEEK 2

Proverbs 2:1–15

WEEK 2

¹ My son, if you receive my words
    and treasure up my commandments with you,
² making your ear attentive to wisdom
    and inclining your heart to understanding;
³ yes, if you call out for insight
    and raise your voice for understanding,
⁴ if you seek it like silver
    and search for it as for hidden treasures,
⁵ then you will understand the fear of the LORD
    and find the knowledge of God.
⁶ For the LORD gives wisdom;
    from his mouth come knowledge and understanding;
⁷ he stores up sound wisdom for the upright;
    he is a shield to those who walk in integrity,
⁸ guarding the paths of justice
    and watching over the way of his saints.
⁹ Then you will understand righteousness and justice
    and equity, every good path;
¹⁰ for wisdom will come into your heart,
    and knowledge will be pleasant to your soul;
¹¹ discretion will watch over you,
    understanding will guard you,
¹² delivering you from the way of evil,
    from men of perverted speech,
¹³ who forsake the paths of uprightness
    to walk in the ways of darkness,

¹⁴ *who rejoice in doing evil*
and delight in the perverseness of evil,
¹⁵ *men whose paths are crooked,*
and who are devious in their ways.

PROVERBS 2:1–15

The Pursuit of Wisdom

Proverbs helps us define wisdom, understand why it is important, and know how to be a person characterized by knowledge and understanding (see Prov. 1:1–7). The *ESV Study Bible* notes that wisdom in Proverbs is best described as "skill in the art of godly living." Highly practical in nature, Proverbs provides us with specific examples of what it looks like to live in a God-honoring way.

This week we will spend time in prayerful study of Proverbs 2:1–15, a passage that encourages us to seek out wisdom so that we are better equipped to understand and obey the Lord's commands. Proverbs 2 also helps us see the way in which the Lord through wisdom protects and guards those he loves.

Day 1

The first five verses of Proverbs 2 emphasize the importance of *actively pursuing* wisdom. God wants us to long for understanding and to seek it out eagerly. Note the *ifs* of verses 1, 3, and 4 followed by the *then* of verse 5. If we crave God's wisdom and passionately run after it, then God will be pleased to honor our efforts.

Verse 1 reveals where our pursuit of wisdom begins: by receiving God's Word and treasuring up his commandments. Through our knowledge of his Word we become *discerning*. Discernment is a concept related closely to wisdom. It is the ability to judge well, to determine the course of wisdom even in confusing, complex, and unsettling situations.

Hebrews 5:14 tells us that "solid food is for the mature, for those who have their powers of discernment trained by constant practice to distinguish good from evil." It is by studying and meditating on Scripture that we are able to discern and hear God's voice over our own and that of the world. Read Proverbs 2:1–5 carefully today, praying over each of the calls to action in these verses.

Day 2

God tells us to seek wisdom, but the Bible makes it equally clear that knowledge and understanding are *gifts* from the one who is "wonderful in counsel and excellent in wisdom" (Isa. 28:29). Proverbs 2:6 teaches that "the LORD gives wisdom; from his mouth come knowledge and understanding."

There is a type of wisdom that comes to us as we age and experience life in all its complexities. The longer we live, the better we become at navigating the challenges that come our way. But human wisdom, based simply on our knowledge of the world around us, is flawed. While such understanding is valuable, we can and do misunderstand, misinterpret, and miscommunicate. We are fallen creatures, and everything that originates with us is susceptible to sin.

This is why we are in desperate need of the true wisdom and understanding that come from God—rooted in his perfect Word and given to us by the Spirit. Meditate today on verse 6. Ask the Lord for a heart and mind receptive to his Word—and for the humility to submit to what he says is wise and good.

Day 3

The phrase "sound wisdom" is found three times in the book of Proverbs (2:7; 3:21; 8:14)—four times if we include the related phrase "sound judgment" (18:1). *Sound* in these instances means *true*, describing wisdom that is based on and aligned with the revelation of God in Scripture. Such wisdom is reserved for—indeed, it is "stored up for"—the "upright" (2:7), for those who love and obey God. Because true wisdom is a gift from God, it is unique to believers.

In the writings of Paul in the New Testament, the word *sound* often precedes the words *doctrine, teaching,* or *speech.* Here the meaning connotes that which is *healthy* and, again, true. *Sound* doctrine is doctrine that is in accord with the gospel of Jesus.

Proverbs 2:7–8 suggests that one way in which God protects ("shields") his people is by equipping them with sound wisdom. In this way God also "guards the paths of justice"—he takes care of and watches over us so that we can in turn care for and watch over others. As we grow in the knowledge of that which is true and healthy, we are able to share that understanding with the world.

Spend time reflecting on Proverbs 2:7–8. The phrase "stores up" in verse 7 indicates that God delights in giving us wisdom—he does not give reluctantly or sparingly but rather he lavishes wisdom on us when we seek and ask him for it. Meditate on that promise today, and ask God for an outpouring of his wisdom.

Day 4

Micah 6:8 is one of the clearest, most succinct teachings in the Bible regarding what pleases the Lord:

> He has told you, O man, what is good;
>> and what does the LORD require of you
> but to do justice, and to love kindness,
>> and to walk humbly with your God?

Here in Proverbs 2:9–10 we find a crucial precursor to that command. If we pursue wisdom, if we seek it out by loving and living by the Word of God, "*then* [we] will understand righteousness and justice and equity, every good path" (v. 9). We will know what justice and kindness look like; we will know where to begin in terms of living a life of obedience. "Wisdom will come" into our hearts, and "knowledge will be pleasant" to our souls (v. 10). As we grow closer and closer to our Lord Jesus, the things that please him will increasingly become the desire of our hearts.

In the *ESV Gospel Transformation Study Bible* Ray Ortlund notes, "True wisdom is not an abstract principle. It is our walk with the living God." As you pray today, ask God to increase your passion for justice and righteousness and to give you the ability to identify "every good path" (v. 9).

Day 5

Our passage ends by reiterating the promise of Proverbs 2:7–8 that the Lord will use wisdom to protect and keep us. Wisdom is a safeguard against those who would harm us spiritually:

> Discretion will watch over you,
>> understanding will guard you,
> delivering you from the way of evil,
>> from men of perverted speech,
> who forsake the paths of uprightness
>> to walk in the ways of darkness,
> who rejoice in doing evil
>> and delight in the perverseness of evil,
> men whose paths are crooked,
>> and who are devious in their ways. (2:11–15)

The Bible does not shy away from declaring as evil those mindsets and actions that are in opposition to God. Galatians 1:4 makes clear that we live in an "evil age." This statement is sobering, as it reminds us, as does Proverbs 2, that evil is alive and active in our world. We cannot be idle.

But, as you pray today, rest in the assurance that God walks with us and guards our hearts and minds by stabilizing and fortifying them with his Word. Read Proverbs 2:1–15 in its entirety today, and ask the Lord again to renew and increase your love for his commandments.

WEEK 3

Daniel 1:17–21

WEEK 3

¹⁷ *As for these four youths, God gave them learning and skill in all literature and wisdom, and Daniel had understanding in all visions and dreams.* ¹⁸ *At the end of the time, when the king had commanded that they should be brought in, the chief of the eunuchs brought them in before Nebuchadnezzar.* ¹⁹ *And the king spoke with them, and among all of them none was found like Daniel, Hananiah, Mishael, and Azariah. Therefore they stood before the king.* ²⁰ *And in every matter of wisdom and understanding about which the king inquired of them, he found them ten times better than all the magicians and enchanters that were in all his kingdom.* ²¹ *And Daniel was there until the first year of King Cyrus.*

DANIEL 1:17-21

Wisdom in the World

Israel and Judah's obstinate refusal to obey God eventually put them under his judgment. For the northern kingdom of Israel this came at the hands of the Assyrian empire, while for the southern kingdom of Judah it came compliments of Babylon. In the sixth century BC King Nebuchadnezzar captured the people of Judah and resettled them in Babylon. He began this deportation in the seventh century by taking the best and brightest, with the intention of assimilating these gifted individuals into Babylonian culture:

> Then the king commanded Ashpenaz, his chief eunuch, to bring some of the people of Israel, both of the royal family and of the nobility, youths without blemish, of good appearance and skillful in all wisdom, endowed with knowledge, understanding learning, and competent to stand in the king's palace, and to teach them the literature and language of the Chaldeans. (Dan. 1:3–4)

Daniel and his three friends—Hananiah, Mishael, and Azariah— were among this first wave of Judeans brought to Babylon. The book of Daniel, written by Daniel himself, is a record of his time in Babylon, which spanned over seventy years.

Although Judah's exile was a result of God's judgment, the Lord's faithfulness to the covenant is evident in his care both for his people and for those holding them captive. Through the prophet Jeremiah God gave his people the following instructions regarding their time in exile:

> Seek the welfare of the city where I have sent you into exile, and pray to the LORD on its behalf, for in its welfare you will find your welfare. (Jer. 29:7)

God promised Abraham in Genesis 12:3 that "in you all the families of the earth shall be blessed." This would include even the people of Babylon. Daniel is one of the best examples in Scripture of God's granting his people wisdom and understanding in order for them to bear witness to him and glorify him among unbelievers.

Day 1

In Daniel 2 Nebuchadnezzar has experienced a nightmare so distressing that he reacts with rage. But Daniel asks to be brought before the king so that he can interpret the dream. Before he does so he and his friends "seek mercy from the God of heaven concerning this mystery" (2:18). The Lord answers the prayer, revealing to Daniel the meaning of Nebuchadnezzar's dream. Daniel responds with praise and thanksgiving:

> Blessed be the name of God forever and ever,
>> to whom belong wisdom and might.
> He changes times and seasons;
>> he removes kings and sets up kings;
> he gives wisdom to the wise
>> and knowledge to those who have understanding;
> he reveals deep and hidden things;
>> he knows what is in the darkness,
>> and the light dwells with him.
> To you, O God of my fathers,
>> I give thanks and praise,
> for you have given me wisdom and might,
>> and have now made known to me what we asked of you,
>> for you have made known to us the king's matter.
>> (Dan. 2:20–23)

God delights in giving his people wisdom and understanding when they humbly ask. He uses these gifts to protect and safeguard us and to care for others who do not yet know him. Read Daniel 1:17–21 carefully today. Ask God to bless your study of this passage this week and to direct your eyes to the words and phrases where he would have you linger and dig deeper. Praise God for his great wisdom and thank him for his willingness to give understanding to his people.

_____

_____

_____

_____

_____

_____

_____

_____

_____

_____

_____

_____

_____

_____

_____

_____

Day 2

It may come as a surprise to us that God not only approved of Daniel and his friends' learning the literature and culture of the Babylonians but went so far as to bless their knowledge in those areas. Daniel 1:20 emphasizes how God gave his servants extensive understanding "in every matter of wisdom and understanding about which the king inquired of them."

In his study on Daniel, Todd Wilson notes,

> Daniel and his three friends display a readiness to engage in the culture and customs of the Babylonians, and yet this clearly has limits. Daniel does not simply accommodate to the host culture of the Babylonians. At the same time, he does show a high degree of acculturation: acquiring both learning and skill in "all literature and wisdom" of the Babylonians (v. 17). This provides a good case study for thinking about the challenge of being in the world, but not of the world (John 17:15–16).

Read Daniel 1:17–21 again today. Highlight words and phrases that stand out to you—particularly repeated themes. Spend time reflecting on God's purposes in granting wisdom and understanding to Daniel and his friends. We will continue to unpack what it means to be "in the world, but not of the world" this week. Ask God for understanding and insight on this crucial theme.

Day 3

Daniel and his friends became experts in the culture of the Babylonians—even more so than the Babylonians themselves (Dan. 1:20)! The four men learned the literature, philosophies, and customs of the land inside and out. And yet the Bible makes it clear that they were not, in fact, assimilated into Babylonian culture in the way in which Nebuchadnezzar had intended. Daniel and his friends remained faithful to the God of Israel.

Daniel 6 offers insight into how this was possible. Even when faced with death if he continued to worship God, Daniel nonetheless "went to his house where he had windows in his upper chamber open toward Jerusalem. He got down on his knees three times a day and prayed and gave thanks before his God, as he had done previously" (6:10). Despite how well Daniel knew the customs and literature of the Babylonians, it is safe to say that he had an even greater knowledge and understanding of God's Word.

Pray today for an increased desire to spend time with the Lord. If, like most of us, you struggle to find time for prayer or Bible study, ask God to help you steward your time well and to find creative ways to spend time with him.

Day 4

Before the crucifixion Jesus prayed what is known as the High Priestly Prayer for his followers. It is from this passage that we glean the concept of being "in but not of the world."

> I do not ask that you take them out of the world, but that you keep them from the evil one. They are not of the world, just as I am not of the world. Sanctify them in the truth; your word is truth. (John 17:15–17)

Daniel and his friends could not have remained faithful to God without his help, and neither can we. Our only hope lies in God's answer to Jesus' prayer for us: he sanctifies us in truth. The *ESV Study Bible* explains,

> The sanctification of Christians is a lifelong process. It involves both a relational component (separation from participating in and being influenced by evil) and a moral component (growth in holiness or moral purity in attitudes, thoughts, and actions). This occurs in the truth, that is, as Christians believe, think, and live according to "the truth" in relation to God, themselves, and the world. This truth comprises the entire Bible, for Jesus says, your word is truth. . . . God's Word does not simply conform to some other external standard of "truth," but . . . is truth itself.

Spend time today thanking God for the gift of sanctification. Ask for increased growth in holiness and Christlikeness.

Day 5

It is challenging to remain faithful to the Lord and his commands in a culture hostile to the things of God. At times we can feel discouraged and disillusioned, wondering whether we can really make a difference when things are this bad. It is easy to think that our current context is one uniquely antagonistic to Christianity.

But the book of Daniel offers us profound encouragement. God delights in using his people as vessels of his mercy and grace in even the bleakest of circumstances. On this side of the cross, those who are in Jesus and indwelled by the Holy Spirit have even more reason to hope! For "the light shines in the darkness, and the darkness has not overcome it" (John 1:5).

Daniel is an admirable figure, for sure, but the focus of the book of Daniel is on God himself. And he is as willing to grant us wisdom and knowledge as he was to Daniel and his friends. Read Daniel 1:17–21 again today. If you are feeling disheartened or weighed down by the state of the world, ask God to use the passage to encourage your soul. Ask him to help you enjoy learning and the pursuit of knowledge and to use those endeavors in such a way that brings him honor and praise.

_____

_____

_____

_____

WEEK 4

Colossians 4:5–6

WEEK 4

⁵ Walk in wisdom toward outsiders, making the best use of the time.
⁶ Let your speech always be gracious, seasoned with salt, so that you
may know how you ought to answer each person.

COLOSSIANS 4:5-6

Walking in Wisdom

In Proverbs 2, which we studied a few weeks ago, we are promised
that if we pursue wisdom, "discretion will watch over [us], understanding will guard [us]" (v. 11)—wisdom will keep us from being
misled or taken in by "men whose paths are crooked, and who are
devious in their ways" (v. 15).

The book of Colossians brings us back to this theme. Paul wrote
to believers at Colossae because he was troubled over false teaching
plaguing the church there. His letter is addressed "to the saints
and faithful brothers in Christ at Colossae" (Col. 1:2). These were
true believers in Jesus, but they were nonetheless at risk of being
deceived by teaching contrary to the gospel.

Paul's desire for his brothers and sisters at Colossae was that
they be filled with the knowledge and wisdom of God in order to
stand firm against false teaching, holding fast to Christ. And so
he prayed that they would

be filled with the knowledge of his will in all spiritual wisdom and understanding, so as to walk in a manner worthy of the Lord, fully pleasing to him: bearing fruit in every good work and increasing in the knowledge of God. (vv. 9–10)

We see in Colossians that wisdom guards us from false teaching. In doing so it benefits both us and those with whom we are in conversation. Through wisdom God protects the hearts and minds of those who love him, and through wisdom he equips us to love others by pointing them to the goodness, truth, and beauty of the gospel. Our passage this week, Colossians 4:5–6, instructs us to "walk in wisdom" so that we might bring the light of Christ to those around us.

Day 1

The Bible often uses the words *walk* and *walking* to describe our relationship with the Lord. Walking with someone implies being close to that person. The word also indicates consistency and regularity. In Deuteronomy 10:12–13, God says to Israel,

> And now, Israel, what does the LORD your God require of you, but to fear the LORD your God, *to walk in all his ways*, to love him, to serve the LORD your God with all your heart and with all your soul, and to keep the commandments and statutes of the LORD, which I am commanding you today for your good?

Our passage this week begins by exhorting us to "walk in wisdom" (Col. 4:5). Wisdom is not something that comes and goes for us on an as-needed basis. Rather, it is something that we pursue passionately and consistently. Doing so is an expression and outworking of our wholehearted obedience to God. Walking in wisdom is part of what it means to "walk in all his ways."

Read Colossians 4:5–6 carefully today. Ask the Lord to help you commit it to memory this week. The passage is short, but it is a powerful reminder of the importance of wisdom. Ask God to use this passage to keep you mindful of the effect your words can have on your hearers.

Day 2

We began our study of wisdom in Deuteronomy 4, where God commands Israel to keep all his statutes and rules when they enter the Promised Land. What is a key reason they are to do so?

> That will be your wisdom and your understanding in the sight of the peoples, who, when they hear all these statutes, will say, "Surely this great nation is a wise and understanding people." (Deut. 4:6)

The New Testament, as well as the Old, is concerned with how the people of God conduct themselves and appear to "outsiders"—those who do not yet know the Lord. First Thessalonians 4:11–12 instructs us to

> aspire to live quietly, and to mind your own affairs, and to work with your hands, . . . so that you may walk properly before outsiders and be dependent on no one.

Why is God concerned about what nonbelievers think of us? Again, Israel's calling, and ours as well, is to reflect him, and, in so doing, to point people to the gospel. One way that we do this, as Colossians 4:5 tells us, is to "walk in wisdom toward outsiders."

Spend time in prayer for particular people in your life who are not yet believers. Ask the Lord to help you live out your faith in such a way that they take notice and ask questions that lead to gospel conversations.

Day 3

Colossians 4:5 tells us that by walking in wisdom we are being equipped to make "the best use of the time." Paul uses similar language in Ephesians 5:15–17, a passage that helps us understand what he means by this phrase:

> Look carefully then how you walk, not as unwise but as wise, making the best use of the time, because the days are evil. Therefore do not be foolish, but understand what the will of the Lord is.

The "days are evil" because Jesus has not yet returned to make all things new, and so the enemy and his forces are still very much at work in the world. First Peter 5:8 warns us to "be sober-minded; be watchful." Why? Because our "adversary the devil prowls around like a roaring lion, seeking someone to devour."

Wisdom recognizes the battlefield we are in the middle of, and in humility it clings to the one person able to guard our hearts and minds. It also joyfully anticipates the day in which Jesus will come back for us, and it longs for others to be able to look forward to that day as well.

Meditate today on what it means to make "the best use of the time" we are given. Ask God to reveal any thoughts, words, or behaviors in your life that fall short of that ideal.

Day 4

A key aspect of wisdom is the ability to communicate effectively and graciously. Colossians 4:6 makes the following exhortation: "Let your speech always be gracious, seasoned with salt." The people we are in conversation with are not always going to agree with what we say. But, even if we seem to be the polar opposite of the person we are communicating with, he or she should nonetheless come away from the conversation struck by *the manner* in which we speak.

Our words must be marked by humility and kindness: "Only such as is good for building up, as fits the occasion, that it may give grace to those who hear" (Eph. 4:29). Wisdom discerns not only the right words to say but also the right way to say them. It keeps us from undermining our message by the way we present it.

The phrase "seasoned with salt" indicates that we should also speak in a way that is captivating to our hearers. As Kent Hughes writes in his commentary on Colossians, it is

> salty, savory, scintillating—not the dull, sanctimonious vocabulary that seems to be demanded in some church circles. It is thoughtful speech, words with content. It is joyful, even witty, for this is what salty speech meant in classical Greek.

As you pray today, ask the Lord to give you wisdom specifically in regard to your speech. Pray that your words will build up others, and be a source of joy and grace in their lives—even if they disagree with you!

Day 5

The theme of 1 Peter 3:15 is strikingly similar to that of Colossians 4:5–6:

> In your hearts honor Christ the Lord as holy, always being prepared to make a defense to anyone who asks you for a reason for the hope that is in you; yet do it with gentleness and respect.

God instructs us to pursue wisdom actively so that we are ready to give a measured, thoughtful response any time we are asked about our faith. We are to be people characterized by gentleness and sound reasoning, known for treating others with respect and dignity. Such characteristics help open doors for sharing the gospel because they invite others to have conversations with us.

In the verses immediately preceding our passage this week Paul asks the church at Colossae to

> pray also for us, that God may open to us a door for the word, to declare the mystery of Christ, on account of which I am in prison—that I may make it clear, which is how I ought to speak. (Col. 4:3–4)

Pray this prayer for yourself today—that God would open doors to share the gospel. Ask for sensitivity to the Spirit's leading, so that you will know what to say when those doors open. Pray that your words would be clear, captivating, and gracious, and that you would "know how you ought to answer each person" (v. 6).

WEEK 5

1 Corinthians 1:18–25

WEEK 5

^{18}For the word of the cross is folly to those who are perishing, but to us who are being saved it is the power of God. ^{19}For it is written,

> *"I will destroy the wisdom of the wise,*
> *and the discernment of the discerning I will thwart."*

^{20}Where is the one who is wise? Where is the scribe? Where is the debater of this age? Has not God made foolish the wisdom of the world? ^{21}For since, in the wisdom of God, the world did not know God through wisdom, it pleased God through the folly of what we preach to save those who believe. ^{22}For Jews demand signs and Greeks seek wisdom, ^{23}but we preach Christ crucified, a stumbling block to Jews and folly to Gentiles, ^{24}but to those who are called, both Jews and Greeks, Christ the power of God and the wisdom of God. ^{25}For the foolishness of God is wiser than men, and the weakness of God is stronger than men.

1 CORINTHIANS 1:18-25

The Wisdom of Christ

Paul's original audience was a church plagued with misunderstanding. The church at Corinth tolerated and even practiced behavior very much at odds with God's commands. First Corinthians was written to provide clear gospel instruction to the church and to encourage unity among the believers.

A significant obstacle Paul had to overcome was Corinth's preoccupation with eloquent speech, or rhetoric. The Corinthians loved communication that was powerful, articulate, and persuasive. In his study on 1 Corinthians Jay Thomas explains,

> Ancient rhetoricians were professional traveling speakers who thrilled crowds with their use of words. Their purpose was to persuade a crowd toward a viewpoint. The viewpoint per se was not crucial, but rather the persuading itself was the point. These speakers used words in such a way as to delight and move their audience. The power was in the words and human giftedness. The rhetorician did not even necessarily need to believe the viewpoint he was advocating.

Paul's audience was more interested in the speaker than the message. But Paul corrects this erroneous way of thinking by telling the Corinthians that he was sent "to preach the gospel, and not with words of eloquent wisdom, lest the cross of Christ be emptied of its power" (1 Cor. 1:17).

In the cross of Jesus God has given us the ultimate example of his words in Isaiah 55:8–9:

> My thoughts are not your thoughts,
>> neither are your ways my ways, declares the LORD.
> For as the heavens are higher than the earth,
>> so are my ways higher than your ways
>> and my thoughts than your thoughts.

Our passage this week shows us the extent to which God in the gospel turns human wisdom on its head.

Day 1

Death by crucifixion was a familiar concept to Paul's audience. But it was so horrific that it was considered an inappropriate subject even to talk about. That *anything* good could come from such an act was absurd by human logic. Thus Paul declares that "the word of the cross is folly to those who are perishing" (1 Cor. 1:18a).

"But to us who are being saved it is the power of God" (v. 18b). By the power of the Spirit those who are in Jesus recognize the cross as the power of God to save them from our sins. Later in 1 Corinthians Paul asks,

> Who knows a person's thoughts except the spirit of that person, which is in him? So also no one comprehends the thoughts of God except the Spirit of God. Now we have received not the spirit of the world, but the Spirit who is from God, that we might understand the things freely given us by God. And we impart this in words not taught by human wisdom but taught by the Spirit, interpreting spiritual truths to those who are spiritual.
>
> The natural person does not accept the things of the Spirit of God, for they are folly to him, and he is not able to understand them because they are spiritually discerned. (1 Cor. 2:11–14)

Read 1 Corinthians 1:18–25 unhurriedly today. This passage is densely packed with theological truth. We can be tempted to rush through it or gloss over it—there is so much to take in. Ask the Lord to help you as you read, to grant you understanding. Spend time reflecting on verse 18 in particular.

Day 2

First Corinthians 1:19 is a reference to Isaiah 29:14, which says,

> Therefore, behold, I will again
> do wonderful things with this people,
> with wonder upon wonder;
> and the wisdom of their wise men shall perish,
> and the discernment of their discerning men shall be
> hidden.

This verse from Isaiah falls within a passage about the siege of Jerusalem, a time when God's people faced judgment for their refusal to honor and obey him. But even in the midst of his judgment God promises that he will be faithful. He will do "wonderful things" with his people, and those things will happen in a way that no one but God could imagine. In the folly of the cross the "wisdom of their wise men" and the "discernment of their discerning men" are proven to be nothing.

In his devotional on 1 Corinthians 1 Dan Doriani writes:

> The gospel . . . presents Jesus, slain in weakness, raised in power. He is a state criminal who, by his humiliating death, defeated death, the Devil, and sin. This defies wisdom. It is a doctrine that no human would conceive. Thus "the cross is folly to those who are perishing," but it is the power of God for the saved.

Read the entire passage again today. Highlight words or phrases that stand out, and meditate on those sections. Spend time praising God for his great wisdom, exemplified perfectly in Jesus.

Day 3

Human wisdom is finite; there are things that we will simply never be able to understand. Our minds have also been tainted by the fall, and so we do not by nature always see things as they truly are. In fact, Romans 1 tells us that because of sin we fail to understand the truth about God that is right in front of us:

> What can be known about God is plain to them, because God has shown it to them. For his invisible attributes, namely, his eternal power and divine nature, have been clearly perceived, ever since the creation of the world, in the things that have been made. So they are without excuse. For although they knew God, they did not honor him as God or give thanks to him, but they became futile in their thinking, and their foolish hearts were darkened. Claiming to be wise, they became fools, and exchanged the glory of the immortal God for images resembling mortal man and birds and animals and creeping things. (Rom. 1:19–23)

The limits of human intellect are humbling, a truth Paul urges us to accept and embrace in 1 Corinthians 1:20–21. Our "wisdom" will never lead us to God—only the folly of the gospel has the power to reconcile us to him.

Mediate today on verses 20–21. There is little we can do in light of these verses but recognize our need for a Savior and rejoice that in Jesus one has been provided. Spend time again in praise and thanksgiving.

Day 4

In 1 Corinthians 1:23–24 Paul addresses the expectations and values of his original audience. Having faced centuries of oppression, the Jewish people expected a messiah who would be formidable and awe-inspiring, a powerful political leader who would free them from the tyranny of Rome. Throughout the Gospels we read that unbelieving Jews constantly demanded signs from Jesus to prove that he was who he said he was, because he certainly looked nothing like the person they were anticipating.

The Greeks, as evidenced by the Corinthians' high valuation of eloquence, viewed reasoning and knowledge as supreme. A messiah who was

> despised and rejected by men,
> > a man of sorrows and acquainted with grief;
> and as one from whom men hide their faces (Isa. 53:3)

was appalling to Jews and ridiculous to Greeks.

One way or the other, God's chosen method of salvation offends everyone! That is, except for "those who are called, both Jews and Greeks," who recognize Jesus as "the power of God and the wisdom of God" (1 Cor. 1:24).

Read verses 23–24 carefully today. Reflect especially on what it means that Christ is the "power of God and the wisdom of God." Savor that truth! Spend time enjoying being in the presence of Jesus, delighting in the fact that through him God has exceeded all our human expectations.

Day 5

As with 1 Corinthians 1:20–21, the final verse of our passage is so humbling that it is almost humorous:

> The foolishness of God is wiser than men, and the weakness of God is stronger than men. (v. 25)

Here we are reminded of the central gospel truth found in Ephesians 2:8–9:

> By grace you have been saved through faith. And this is not your own doing; it is the gift of God, not a result of works, so that no one may boast.

God alone saves, and God alone determines and establishes wisdom. First Corinthians 1 ends with a strong admonition against placing one's confidence in earthly wisdom:

> Consider your calling, brothers: not many of you were wise according to worldly standards, not many were powerful, not many were of noble birth. But God chose what is foolish in the world to shame the wise; God chose what is weak in the world to shame the strong; God chose what is low and despised in the world, even things that are not, to bring to nothing things that are, so that no human being might boast in the presence of God. And because of him you are in Christ Jesus, who became to us wisdom from God, righteousness and sanctification and redemption, so that, as it is written, "Let the one who boasts, boast in the Lord." (1 Cor. 1:26–31)

For those of us who love Jesus, our utter dependence on him is the source of great joy and assurance. As you pray today, read 1 Corinthians 1:18–25 in its entirety again, carefully. Rest and rejoice in the sufficiency and power of Jesus.

WEEK 6

James 3:13–18

WEEK 6

13 Who is wise and understanding among you? By his good conduct let him show his works in the meekness of wisdom. 14 But if you have bitter jealousy and selfish ambition in your hearts, do not boast and be false to the truth. 15 This is not the wisdom that comes down from above, but is earthly, unspiritual, demonic. 16 For where jealousy and selfish ambition exist, there will be disorder and every vile practice. 17 But the wisdom from above is first pure, then peaceable, gentle, open to reason, full of mercy and good fruits, impartial and sincere. 18 And a harvest of righteousness is sown in peace by those who make peace.

JAMES 3:13–18

The Wisdom from Above

In John 3:3 Jesus baffles Nicodemus by telling him, "Truly, truly, I say to you, unless one is born again he cannot see the kingdom of God." Nicodemus's bewilderment should not surprise us—Jesus' statement is shocking. But many of us, perhaps especially those of us who came to know the Lord at an early age, have heard the phrase "born again" so often that we are not appropriately jarred by it.

The Bible says that we must be born again because we are dead in our sins:

God, being rich in mercy, because of the great love with which he loved us, even when we were dead in our trespasses, made us alive together with Christ—by grace you have been saved. (Eph. 2:4–5)

When we come to Jesus, he brings us from death to life. He turns us into someone entirely new:

If anyone is in Christ, he is a new creation. The old has passed away; behold, the new has come. (2 Cor. 5:17)

Colossians 1:13 tells us that God "has delivered us from the domain of darkness and transferred us to the kingdom of his beloved Son." The spectacular change that occurs for those of us who are in Jesus is emphasized throughout the New Testament, but it is never unpacked more clearly than in the book of James. The book's key theme can be summarized like this: if you have truly been born again, then that transformation is so dramatic that your actions and your way of thinking will necessarily reflect this new birth.

James is one of the most instructive books in the Bible regarding what it looks like to be a follower of Jesus. And in our passage this week we will see that one of the key characteristics of a Christian is a heart of God-given wisdom, equipping us to live lives of obedience.

Day 1

In Luke 6:45 Jesus tells us, "The good person out of the good treasure of his heart produces good, and the evil person out of his evil treasure produces evil, for out of the abundance of the heart his mouth speaks." James emphasizes this truth by contrasting true wisdom with the wisdom of the world. Godly wisdom is a result of the sanctifying work of the Spirit, and it looks vastly different from the "wisdom" that flows from hearts that have not been set free from sin's grasp.

In his book *Radically Whole* David Gibson writes this concerning the book of James:

> This whole letter is about getting wise. It is wisdom for foolish Christians and foolish churches, and if we want to fix what ails us, we don't just need to fix our words or our actions, but we must also recalibrate our hearts with wisdom.
>
> When things go wrong in a church, or in the world, we so often look for quick solutions. Do A, not B; stop doing that; start doing this. We look for actions that will fix things, but it is James's settled conviction that outward actions need to flow from a wise heart.

Read James 3:13–18 carefully in its entirety today. Ask the Lord to sanctify you so that wise words and behavior overflow from your heart.

Day 2

There is an inseparable connection between humility and wisdom, which we see often in the book of James. In James 3:13 James identifies those who are truly "wise and understanding" by means of the striking phrase "meekness of wisdom."

The Greek word rendered "meekness" is the same word translated "gentleness" when listed among the fruit of the Spirit in Galatians 5:23. And in Matthew 5:5 Jesus teaches, "Blessed are the meek, for they shall inherit the earth." The word *meek* has fallen out of use today, and, when it is used, it is often meant to indicate that someone is timid. But Scripture uses the word quite differently, and the link to humility is clear.

The meek person according to the Bible is one who has humbled himself before the Lord—who neither trusts in his own strength nor looks out primarily for his own good, but who gladly submits to and depends on the Lord. The *ESV Study Bible* notes that "meekness comes not from cowardice or passivity but rather from trusting God and therefore being set free from anxious self-promotion."

Mediate today on James 3:13. Godly wisdom cannot exist without humility. Ask the Lord to help you grow in the "meekness of wisdom."

Day 3

Words and conduct that originate in "bitter jealousy and selfish ambition," rather than humility and gentleness, produce the evil Jesus warns of in Luke 6:45. Evil on the inside produces evil on the outside. It is "earthly, unspiritual, demonic" (James 3:15) and produces "disorder and every vile practice" (v. 16).

Wisdom's purpose is to equip us to love and obey God faithfully and to love others and point them to Jesus. This is possible only when our wisdom is rooted in humble submission to God and an eagerness to promote the well-being of others. The characteristics identified in verses 14–15—"bitter jealousy and selfish ambition"—stand in direct opposition to the wisdom of God. The vivid words in these verses reflect just how high the stakes are.

Reflect today on verses 14–16. And consider how in Ephesians 4:22–24 we are told to

> put off your old self, which belongs to your former manner of life and is corrupt through deceitful desires, and to be renewed in the spirit of your minds, and to put on the new self, created after the likeness of God in true righteousness and holiness.

Pray this verse from Ephesians back to God—ask him to renew your mind and to help cast off remnants of your pre-Christian life and to put on instead the holiness of Jesus.

Day 4

"Wisdom from above" (James 3:17) is recognizable because it is marked by characteristics that begin in Jesus rather than in us. When we display such wisdom, it is evidence of the Spirit's work in our lives.

> The wisdom from above is first pure, then peaceable, gentle, open to reason, full of mercy and good fruits, impartial and sincere. (v. 17)

Wisdom from above begins with *purity*; a heart that has been cleansed of sin and is thus capable of putting others first and of actively seeking their good. The traits that follow display humility and promote kindness. Being right and winning arguments is not the goal of true wisdom. Rather, we can identify wisdom from above by its concern for the spiritual, emotional, and physical welfare of those God has put in our sphere of influence.

Prayerfully reflect on each of the characteristics of true wisdom found in verse 17. Try to memorize this verse. Ask the Lord to call it to your mind when you find yourself in a disagreement with another person. Ask that your response would be marked by these traits rather than by those identified in verse 16.

_____

_____

_____

_____

Day 5

Earlier in his letter James wrote:

> Know this, my beloved brothers: let every person be quick to
> hear, slow to speak, slow to anger; for the anger of man does
> not produce the righteousness of God. (1:19–20)

The "righteousness of God" here refers to that which is pleasing to
God, that which is in accord with what he says is good and right.
As with "bitter jealousy and selfish ambition" (3:14), anger does
not lead anywhere good. The consequences both for the angry
person and for his neighbors are destructive.

But in the final verse of our passage this week, verse 18, we see
the fruit of godly wisdom:

> A harvest of righteousness is sown in peace by those who
> make peace.

Those who are agents of peace—those who are "gentle, open
to reason, full of mercy and good fruits, impartial and sincere"
(v. 17)—will see a "harvest of righteousness."

Carefully read James 3:13–18 again today. Meditate on verse 17,
reflecting on it in light of all the passages we have prayerfully
studied over the past few weeks. Ask the Lord again for a heart
of wisdom that overflows onto those around you, bringing peace,
clarity, comfort, and joy to everyone with whom you interact. Ask
God to help you sow a "harvest of righteousness."

WEEK 6 · DAY 5

For Further Reflection

⁹And so, from the day we heard, we have not ceased to pray for you, asking that you may be filled with the knowledge of his will in all spiritual wisdom and understanding, ¹⁰so as to walk in a manner worthy of the Lord, fully pleasing to him: bearing fruit in every good work and increasing in the knowledge of God; ¹¹being strengthened with all power, according to his glorious might, for all endurance and patience with joy; ¹²giving thanks to the Father, who has qualified you to share in the inheritance of the saints in light. ¹³He has delivered us from the domain of darkness and transferred us to the kingdom of his beloved Son, ¹⁴in whom we have redemption, the forgiveness of sins.

COLOSSIANS 1:9–14

Bibliography

Doriani, Dan. "The Wisdom of God." In *ESV Women's Study Bible*. Wheaton, IL: Crossway, 2020.

ESV Gospel Transformation Study Bible. Wheaton, IL: Crossway, 2018.

ESV Study Bible. Wheaton, IL: Crossway, 2008.

Gibson, David. *Radically Whole: Gospel Healing for the Divided Heart*. Wheaton, IL: Crossway, 2022.

Hughes, R. Kent. *Philippians, Colossians, and Philemon: The Fellowship of the Gospel and the Supremacy of Christ*. Preaching the Word. Wheaton, IL: Crossway, 2013.

Thomas, Jay. *1 Corinthians: A 12-Week Study*. Knowing the Bible. Wheaton, IL: Crossway, 2015.

Wilson, Todd. *Daniel: A 12-Week Study*. Knowing the Bible. Wheaton, IL: Crossway, 2015.

P R A Y E R   J O U R N A L S

ESV Prayer Journals guide your study of a
foundational Scripture topic over 30 days and
create space for writing and prayer—turning your
quiet time into a meditation on God's Word.

For more information, visit **crossway.org/PrayerJournals**.